With examples drawn from actual trials,
here is an introduction to the state and
federal courts of the United States.

All About Courts
and the Law

allabout
books

All About COURTS and the LAW

by Ruth Brindze

illustrated by Leonard Slonevsky

foreword by Erwin N. Griswold

Random House/New York

Contents

Foreword

In the United States, we have many governmental bodies, federal, state, and local. Generally speaking, these are divided into three groups. Our legislatures make the basic laws. The executive branch of the government administers the law. And the judicial branch interprets and applies the law. Good citizenship requires an understanding of all of these functions of government. This book gives an introduction in clear and accurate terms to the system of courts which we have established for the administration of justice, at all levels.

Courts are essential to the maintenance of law and order through their actions in enforcing the law, and in the resolution of disputes which arise between people. In simple countries, justice could be administered by the king, sitting under a tree by the side of the road, using his own good judgment and common sense. But as nations become larger and more complex, this sort of personal justice will not do. We must have justice according to law. Of course, justice must be administered by men. But if justice is to be a reality, these men must follow fair procedures, and must act in accordance with law. For this purpose, we must have a legal profession to aid in the administration of the law, and from which the judges may be chosen. And we must have law schools in which the lawyers and judges can receive their preliminary training.

As this book shows, there are many types of courts. Some of our courts, like the traffic courts, are close to the people, and deal with thousands of cases. Other courts, no less important in the over-all structure, proceed more formally, and deal with more serious matters, civil and criminal. At the apex of our court system is the Supreme Court of the United States, which sits in Washington. This Court makes the ultimate decisions on great and complex Constitutional questions. In many respects, it is the basic guardian of our liberties. It helps all of the other courts in acting as the protectors of society and in the enforcement of our laws.

Miss Brindze has described these courts and shown the kinds of cases they deal with, and how they operate. If society is to function effectively, its members must have respect for the courts, and must comply with their decisions. In order to do this, it is necessary to have an understanding of the courts and their place in our governmental structure. This book provides solid information on which such an understanding may be developed.

"Justice, Sir, is the great interest of man on earth." In these words, Daniel Webster expressed the central place which the administration of justice necessarily holds in any organized society. And, more recently, Judge Learned Hand said: "If we are to keep our democracy, there must be one commandment: Thou shalt not ration justice." If these words are to be more than empty statements, we must all endeavor to perform our duties as citizens, and to understand and support the courts.

Erwin N. Griswold

DEAN, HARVARD LAW SCHOOL

All About Courts
and the Law

Courts and the Law

If the entire world were inhabited by only one man, there would be no need for laws of any kind. Whatever he decided to do would affect only himself.

But when people live together, there is only one sure way to protect the rights of each person, as well as the rights of the group as a whole. That sure way is by setting up *laws*—or rules—and a system for enforcing them.

Not only policemen but also courts are needed to make laws effective. Courts of law—or courts of justice, as they are often called—are the umpires of the rules of law governing our way of life.

The umpire of a ball game bases his decision on what he sees. Without an umpire, ball teams would spend more time arguing and fighting than playing.

Judges who preside in courts of law do not see a crime being committed. Nor do they watch an accident that leads to a lawsuit. In umpiring legal questions, courts base their decisions on the facts presented during a trial.

In ancient times, cruel (and absurd) trials were conducted to determine whether a person was guilty or innocent. For instance, an accused person might be ordered to thrust his arm into a bucket filled with boiling water. If his skin was scalded, as it usually was, the suspect was supposed to be guilty.

Now a fair trial, according to law, is guaranteed in all the courts of our nation. The Constitution of the United States, our most important law, provides basic safeguards intended to assure justice to all.

Strict rules regulate court procedure. There are limits to the questions that may be asked. People who are telling their story to the court must keep to the facts. The rules are designed to make trials fair.

Although courts deal with a great variety of problems, they all fit into one of two classifications —*criminal cases* and *civil cases.*

In a criminal case, a person is accused by the government of having done something that the law states is a crime. Criminal laws forbid acts that may harm any of us—or, in other words, society in general. Because crimes are often sensational, a considerable amount of news is reported about criminal trials. When men accused of robbing a bank are being tried, news accounts resemble a detective story. Detailed descriptions are given about the robbery and how detectives tracked down the men accused of having committed it.

Actually there are many more civil than criminal

cases. However, comparatively few trials of civil cases are reported in newspapers because usually they directly affect only the people involved. Civil laws protect the private rights of individuals.

For instance, suppose one car runs into another, injuring the people in the second car. The injured people have the right to go to court and ask that the driver who was at fault be ordered to pay them a sum of money called *damages*. This is a civil case.

Or suppose the owner of a shoe store contracts with a manufacturer for five dozen pairs of shoes. The manufacturer fails to deliver the shoes. The store owner may start a civil action against the manufacturer. Under civil law a judge may order the manufacturer to pay damages to the store owner.

Many of the laws stating what we should and should not do were developed in England long before the colonists came to America. These laws were brought to the colonies, and after the Declaration of Independence they became the foundation for the legal system of the United States.

Each of the thirteen American colonies had had

its own courts. These became state courts. But the federal government also needed courts to apply national laws, and to deal with situations which could not be handled by the courts of any one state.

Could state courts and federal courts function independently and yet as a team? A plan was worked out to achieve this result. Ordinarily state courts interpret and apply state laws, and federal courts, located throughout the nation, interpret and apply federal laws. They also settle disputes between citizens of different states.

State and federal courts operate side by side, each carrying out its separate duties.

In most cases, decisions of state courts are final. But if a person claims that a state court has denied him a right granted by the federal Constitution, the state court's decision may be reviewed and changed by the Supreme Court of the United States. The Supreme Court is the top court in the federal system and the highest court of our nation.

Laws passed by Congress and by state lawmaking bodies are called *statutes* or *statutory laws*. Some statutes command us to do, or not to do, certain things.

It is a federal crime to counterfeit money because Congress has passed a law stating that counterfeiting is a crime. Boys and girls below a certain age may not drive an automobile because states have laws regulating drivers' licenses. (The age required for a license varies from state to state because each has its own laws.) Everyone who

earns more than a certain amount of money must, under federal law, pay an income tax to the United States. In states with income-tax laws, a tax is also payable to the state. All of these laws are statutes.

There are other statutes which specify how things

are to be done. Some statutes direct the way our government is to operate. A state's department of education is established by a statute. Businessmen who wish to organize a corporation or a partnership must follow the form set forth in a statute. Other statutory laws tell us who can perform marriage ceremonies, how a person can change his name, at what age a boy or girl may leave school to go to work.

Local laws passed by the lawmaking body of a city or town are usually called *ordinances*. A rule made by a governmental department or bureau is generally called a *regulation*. A city water department faced with a possible water shortage may issue a regulation forbidding restaurants to serve water to customers unless a glass of water is requested.

Ordinarily one thinks that legislators are responsible for writing our laws, and that courts are responsible for applying them. But courts are also lawmakers. They make law when deciding cases. Court-made law is called the *common law* or *case law*.

Often courts are faced with problems to which no law applies. If a judge had to decide such problems in the way that he alone believed to be right, everything would depend on the wisdom of just one man. To operate courts in this way would be dangerous. Cases involving similar questions might be decided in one way by Judge A and in another way by Judge B.

Courts therefore use previous decisions of similar problems as a guide. The earlier decisions establish the law. Some of the common law applied by our courts today was established by decisions of English judges who lived long before the American colonies were founded.

Of course, the common law may be changed to make it fit new conditions. Legislators may pass a statute changing the common law. Or a judge may change it when deciding a case. When the highest court of a state gives a new interpretation of an old rule, it changes the law for that state. When the United States Supreme Court gives a new interpretation, it changes the law for the entire nation.

Important new decisions are published each

week in paper-covered books. Later the decisions are reprinted in sturdily bound volumes. There are thousands and thousands of such books. Each state has its own. In addition there are other sets of books containing decisions by federal courts.

A California lawyer generally does his research in books containing the laws and decisions of California courts. A Massachusetts lawyer uses Massachusetts law books. But lawyers all over the United States use the same books when looking up federal laws or decisions of federal court judges.

Lawyers must be good at research. Books are their basic tools. Unless a lawyer keeps up to date with court decisions, he cannot do a good job in advising a client or in presenting his case in court. Even though many lawyers have remarkable memories, they must know how, and where, to find information needed for the problem on which they are working.

For example, an inventor consults a lawyer about the procedure for protecting an invention. The lawyer does research in books containing the law on patents. The books tell how the invention may be registered with the federal government so that, for many years, the invention may be manufactured only by the inventor or with his consent.

The inventor, who wishes to go into business with another man to manufacture the new invention, now asks the lawyer to prepare a partnership agreement. Before drafting the agreement the lawyer may devote a long time to studying provisions of the law of partnership.

The inventor's lawyer suggests that the other man should also be represented by a lawyer. When a contract is being prepared, it is usual for each person to have his own lawyer, who makes sure that the agreement is fair to his client.

Some lawyers hardly ever go to court. They spend most of their time advising clients on legal matters and drawing up necessary documents. Other lawyers specialize in arguing cases in court. They must also do intensive research when preparing a case for trial.

Qualifying to be a lawyer takes hard work. In former times many people prepared for a legal career by working in law offices and reading law books. Abraham Lincoln learned law this way. Now most men and women who wish to become lawyers go first to college and then spend years studying in law school. After graduation they must pass a stiff examination given by the state in which they plan to practice their profession. They must also provide proof of their good character.

A solemn ceremony is conducted when lawyers are "admitted," or authorized, to practice law. A judge of one of the high courts of the state presides. The new lawyers take an oath that they will do nothing inconsistent with truth and honor.

In many courts there is a bar or railing dividing the section reserved for the judge and jury from the rest of the room. In accordance with tradition, lawyers stand in front of the bar when presenting a case. Lawyers are therefore known as members of the Bar.

When a lawyer is elected or appointed to a judgeship, he becomes a member of the Bench. Although a judge's chair is usually comfortable, often upholstered with leather, it is called the *bench*.

Only a lawyer may represent another person in court. But anyone may plead his own case if he wishes to do so. Even a person accused of murder may defend himself. This is rarely done. But there are some courts in which it is customary for a person to handle his own case.

Drivers summoned to court for traffic violations are rarely represented by lawyers. Usually only a fine is at stake, so people do not go to the expense of hiring a lawyer.

Yet a trial for a traffic violation follows the same general form used in all criminal courts. The legal action begins with the issuance of a *summons*—an official notice that a law has been violated and that the person named must appear in court on a certain day. At the trial the officer who issued the summons takes the stand and testifies as to what the driver did. Then the driver tells his version of the incident. Both the officer and the driver may bring witnesses to testify as to the facts.

For anyone who wishes to see a court in action, watching the trial of traffic-law violators is a good way to begin.

Traffic Court

"TRAFFIC COURT: PART ONE" announce the large, black letters on the door of the courtroom. The room is on the main floor of New York City's Criminal Court Building. It is appropriate that the traffic court be located in this building, for the violation of a traffic regulation is a type of crime.

Part One is the court where drivers who are pleading guilty are sentenced. In a criminal case, no trial is conducted if the defendant pleads guilty. The only problem for the judge is what the penalty should be.

A few of the men and women in the crowded courtroom have filed pleas of not guilty, and will be given a full trial at a later date. They have been directed to wait in the courtroom until a trial date is arranged.

"Order in the court," an attendant calls out. "Everybody rise." The judge enters the courtroom and walks rapidly to his desk. He is wearing a long black robe with wide sleeves.

As soon as the judge is seated, the court attendant motions that everyone should sit down. Then he begins to read a list of names. The people whose names are called form a line at the side of the room. This system of lining up people awaiting sentence is used to save time in this court. On an average day, hundreds of traffic violators must be dealt with. In smaller communities, where a judge has fewer cases, each driver is called to come forward separately.

Although all the people in the line are pleading

guilty, each has an explanation for his traffic-law violation. Each defendant hopes that his explanation will persuade the judge either to excuse the violation or to impose a low fine.

Fines for violations of traffic laws are based on an official schedule. However it is up to the judge to decide in each case whether to impose the lowest permitted fine or the highest—or one in between.

The first person in the line is a handsomely dressed woman. She is told to come to the judge's desk. Then an officer of the court reads the offense with which the woman is charged: speeding on a highway. According to the policeman's report the driver was traveling at 53 miles an hour. The speed limit on the highway is 40 miles per hour.

The judge looks stern. He says that by speeding the woman endangered not only herself but also everyone else on the road. Then he asks, "Why did you do it?"

The woman says that she entered the highway only a few miles before the motorcycle policeman stopped her. Previously she had been on a highway with a 60-mile-per-hour speed limit.

"Your Honor, I had been driving for hours at sixty," the woman says, "and I thought I had slowed down sufficiently."

"No excuse," says the judge. "There were signs telling you the speed limit. Twenty-five-dollar fine."

The woman goes to a desk in a corner of the courtroom, where she pays the fine. Her operator's license is stamped with a record of the conviction.

A man with crutches is the next person to come before the judge. His offense was parking too near a street corner. The man admits that he is guilty. He hands a green identification card to a court attendant, who passes it up to the judge. Many communities issue identification cards which entitle disabled persons to special parking privileges. The man explains that he parked for only a short time while attending to business in a nearby building.

"You should have had this card displayed on the inside of the car's windshield," the judge states. "This time I'll let you off."

A boy of about nineteen is the next to tell his story to the judge.

"The officer said I was carrying an illegal num-

ber of passengers. There were two of them, and I drive a car with only two bucket seats. But, Your Honor, the second passenger wasn't in my way. We had been at a party, and when my friends asked for a lift I couldn't refuse, could I?"

"You should have," the judge says curtly. "You broke a law that I consider particularly important. A motor vehicle cannot be operated safely when it is overcrowded. Fifteen-dollar fine."

A man on the court's staff now enters the courtroom. The judge gives him permission to speak. The court officer says: "All persons who have pleaded not guilty and are awaiting trial dates, follow me."

He leads the way into an office where each person is given a choice of several dates for his trial. The earliest date is a month ahead. In large cities where traffic courts are very busy, trials must be arranged far in advance.

The dates suggested to each driver are days on which the policeman who issued the summons will have time off from his other duties and can come to court. The law requires that every person accused of lawbreaking be faced in court by the witness against him.

Two of the drivers—one a woman, the other a man—choose the same date. When they arrive at the courtroom on the trial date, the policemen who are to take part in the trials are waiting outside. Just before the court session is to begin, the policemen enter the courtroom and take seats in the front row.

The first case is *People versus Mary Jones. Versus* is the Latin word for "against." It is usually written in abbreviated form as *vs.* or *v.*

In traffic cases—as in those involving more serious crimes—the offense is considered to have been committed against the public. The case is therefore brought in the name of the People. In some states, criminal cases are brought in the name of the State.

When Mrs. Jones hears her name called she stands up and answers, "Present." The judge asks her to take a seat at the front of the courtroom.

"I want you to hear every word the officer says," the judge remarks.

A court attendant reads the official statement of the accusation against Mrs. Jones.

Then the judge motions the policeman to the witness chair. Before sitting down the policeman gives his name, the number of his police badge, and the station to which he is attached. The information is noted by the court stenographer. At most trials an official stenographer makes an exact record of every word spoken.

While the policeman remains standing, the judge directs him to raise his right hand and asks, "Do you swear to tell the truth, the whole truth, and nothing but the truth, so help you God?"

"I do," says the policeman.

Everyone who testifies in any court is required to take an oath or to affirm to tell the truth.

The policeman's testimony is brief. He refers frequently to a notebook to refresh his memory. Most policemen keep notebooks so that if called to testify months after they have given a summons or made an arrest, they will be able to supply detailed information.

According to the policeman, Mrs. Jones had

failed to obey a stop sign. The police car was parked twenty-five yards from the sign, the officer states, and he had a clear view of the crossing.

"Any questions?" the judge asks Mrs. Jones.

Everyone who testifies in court may be *cross-examined*—questioned—about the facts he has stated. A judge may question a witness while he is giving his testimony. The opposing side is given an opportunity to cross-examine a witness after he completes his testimony.

When Mrs. Jones replies that she has no questions, the policeman steps down from the witness chair. Mrs. Jones takes his place.

Mrs. Jones starts by saying that she has a vivid recollection of everything that happened. It had been raining heavily and there was a traffic tie-up on the highway. As soon as she saw an exit, Mrs. Jones says, she turned off the highway.

"Where did you come to a full stop?" the judge asks.

"As soon as I left the highway," is the response. "I came to a dead stop at the stop sign."

The judge interrupts, "Where was that sign?"

Mrs. Jones tries to recall. She says the sign was at the beginning of the leadout from the highway.

"I told the officer I had done nothing wrong," Mrs. Jones says indignantly.

The judge says patiently that Mrs. Jones's remarks to the policeman have no bearing on the situation. When Mrs. Jones says a friend was riding with her and had seen her come to a full stop, the judge asks whether the witness is prepared to testify.

"She's here," says Mrs. Jones.

The judge tells an attendant to bring the witness into the courtroom. Witnesses are often kept outside a courtroom to prevent them from hearing the testimony given by others. Thus one witness is not influenced by what another says.

Mrs. Jones's friend is a poor witness. First she says the car was stopped at a traffic light, then corrects herself and says that it was a stop sign where the car was stopped. She adds that the sign had a street name on it.

The judge remarks that street names are not lettered on stop signs. He then directs the policeman to take the witness stand again.

"Officer, will you tell me the location of the stop sign?"

"There is a long leadout from the highway, approximately 500 feet long. The sign is located at the end of the leadout."

"Officer, are you regularly assigned to that section of the highway?" the judge asks.

"Yes, I have had that assignment for seven months and have passed that sign many times a day."

"Please step down," the judge says to the policeman and then continues. "I believe the testimony of the officer as to the location of the sign." The judge then pronounces his decision in the following form: "Upon all the evidence presented I find that the People have proved their case beyond a reasonable doubt. I pronounce you guilty. Five-dollar fine."

Mrs. Jones pays the fine to a court attendant, and her conviction is recorded on her license. The trial has lasted about forty-five minutes.

The second case called is *People v. Stuart Leroy*.

Leroy and the policeman who gave him the summons both answer, "Present." Leroy is charged with illegal parking.

The policeman says that Leroy parked his truck too near a school. He also states that there was a no-parking sign about 150 feet from where the truck was left.

When the policeman completes his brief testimony, the judge turns to Leroy and asks, "Any questions?"

"One question," Leroy says as he rises. "Weren't the signs changed a few days after you gave me the ticket?"

The policeman replies that the signs had been changed.

What seemed at the outset to be a simple case of illegal parking is becoming complicated.

Leroy states at the beginning of his testimony that he works for the Post Office. However, he was driving a truck without the official Post Office seal. The account Leroy gives is very exact. He was driving north on Tenth Avenue and turned into Twenty-sixth Street, where he was to make a delivery. Near the corner he saw a sign saying "Parking Prohibited Before 10 A.M." Leroy arrived at Twenty-sixth Street at 11:30. He proceeded about two-thirds of the way down the street and parked. He says that he saw another sign at the far corner but assumed it said the same as the one he had passed and read. Not until he found the ticket on his car did he walk down to read the second sign. It said, "No Parking."

"The week after I got the ticket my route was again down Twenty-sixth Street," Leroy continues, "and I saw that the signs had been changed. There were six signs, not two as there had been on the day I was ticketed. Every one of the signs said 'No Parking.'"

"A situation like this does not arise frequently," the judge declares. "Some people might say that you should have taken the precaution of reading the second sign before leaving your truck. But I think you should be excused for not doing so."

The judge then says, "On all the evidence, I find the defendant not guilty."

Sometimes a judge decides, after hearing the

policeman's account, that no traffic law was violated. In such cases, the driver is not asked to give his version of the incident. Since no law was broken, there is no reason to continue with the trial.

In one case a driver tried to avoid a traffic jam by going through a gas station at the corner. The policeman gave the driver a summons for reckless driving.

"That is obviously not reckless driving," the judge said. "Nothing you have said indicates that this man was driving recklessly. Case dismissed."

If a driver is found guilty and believes that the judge's interpretation of the law is wrong, he may appeal to a higher court—known as an *appellate court*—to review the decision. The right to appeal is one of the most important safeguards of our court system. Few decisions of traffic courts are appealed because, from a practical viewpoint, asking for a review is not worthwhile. The penalty for a traffic violation is usually a fine, and the fine may be far less than the cost of an appeal.

In criminal cases, most appeals involve serious crimes for which the penalty may be a long term in prison, or even the death sentence. In civil cases, the individual who loses in a trial court may decide —when a large sum is at stake—that it is worth spending time and money to ask that the case be reviewed by an appellate court.

A $10,000 Lawsuit

In the city of Utica, as in many other communities, sledding is forbidden except on certain hills. These hills are usually blocked off from automobile traffic. The purpose of restricting coasting to certain areas is to prevent accidents. Sleds and automobiles on the same street are a dangerous combination. It may not be possible for a driver to stop his car quickly enough to avoid hitting a sled that suddenly shoots in front of his automobile.

John Frazier was injured in such an accident. The driver of the car, a young man named Reinman, took the boy to a hospital. The doctor who examined John said that his collar bone was broken. He also had cuts on his head. John spent three weeks at the hospital before he was permitted to go home.

John's mother believed that Reinman should be made to pay for the accident. Under civil law, a person who is hurt because of someone else's negligence—that is, carelessness—has a right to collect a sum of money as damages. The lawyer Mrs. Frazier consulted agreed to try to collect for John. He said he wished to talk to John to hear his story of the accident.

One of the questions the lawyer asked John was how many boys were coasting on Jason Street on the day of the accident. He also asked their names. These boys might make valuable witnesses.

The notes the lawyer made while talking to John were filed in a large envelope labeled *Frazier v. Reinman*. In most civil cases the name of the per-

son who brings suit—that is, starts the action—is given first. He is the *plaintiff*. The person who is sued (in this case Reinman) is the *defendant*.

It certainly would not be justice if everyone injured in an accident were permitted to put the blame on the other party and collect money from him. Generally the plaintiff must prove that the defendant was at fault. But the plaintiff cannot win if his own negligence contributed to the accident.

Some courts deal with small claims, and other courts with larger claims. John sued for $10,000. The case, therefore, went to the highest trial court of New York State.

In a case such as John's there is usually a choice between a jury trial and having a judge alone make the decision. John's lawyer asked for a jury trial.

Because of the great number of accident cases that come to court, there may be a long wait before such a lawsuit is tried. The trial of John's case began a little more than a year after the accident.

In court the first task was to select twelve jurors. Although each state has its own law as to how many people are required for a trial jury, twelve is the usual number. All male citizens between certain ages (except those excused for special reasons) may be called upon to serve as jurors. In many states women are also eligible for jury duty. From the group of men and women called for jury duty, lawyers choose those whom they believe are best for their particular case. Many questions may be asked before a lawyer accepts a man or woman as a juror. Days are sometimes spent before a jury is chosen.

In the case of *Frazier v. Reinman* the selection of the jury was completed in about an hour. After the twelve men had taken their places in the jury box, the judge said, "The jury will rise to be sworn." They took the oath to give a verdict according to the law and the evidence.

Then John's lawyer addressed the court. He started in the traditional way, saying, "May it please the Court, gentlemen of the jury." He then gave a brief summary of the accident and said that he would prove it had been caused solely by the driver's carelessness.

Next the defendant's lawyer addressed the court. He would prove, he stated, that Reinman was not at fault.

After these opening statements, John's lawyer called as his first witness the doctor who had treated the boy when he was brought to the hospital.

Witnesses do not make long speeches. They answer questions posed by the lawyers. When a lawyer is examining his own witness, he tries for answers that will produce the most favorable impression. A lawyer's purpose is just the opposite when cross-examining a witness for the other side.

John's lawyer asked the doctor only a few questions about John's injuries and the treatment that had been given. Then Reinman's lawyer cross-examined the doctor. The questions asked during the cross-examination were designed to show that John had not been badly injured and that he had made a complete recovery.

The second witness was John himself.

The first question his lawyer asked was, "John, how old are you?"

"Twelve years old."

The next questions were about the school John attended and his class.

If John was to win his case it was important to convince the jury that, even though Jason Street was not a legal coasting area, it was regularly used for sledding. John's lawyer therefore asked whether other boys were sliding down Jason Street hill on the day of the accident. The question seemed innocent enough, but the defendant's lawyer immediately jumped up and said that he objected to it. The lawyer wanted the judge to rule that John should not answer the question. But the judge refused to rule that the question should be withdrawn.

John was questioned in detail about what he had done when he saw the car, whether his sled was hit on the right or left side, and so on. Finally John's lawyer said he had completed his examination. The defendant's lawyer then started his cross-examination.

Many of the questions he asked seemed to be repetitions of the ones John had just answered. But they had different twists and angles. The cross-examination was conducted quietly. In plays and movies there is often a good deal of shouting during a cross-examination. But in a real trial lawyers usually speak in a low voice and act with the utmost politeness.

After the defendant's lawyer finished his questions, John's lawyer asked a few additional ones. His purpose was to convince the jurors that John had done nothing to contribute to the accident. The purpose of the defendant's lawyer was just the opposite.

The third witness was a boy who had been on Jason Street hill on the day of the accident. When this witness was cross-examined, the defendant's lawyer asked, "You have seen a policeman up in that section, haven't you, when you boys were sliding?"

"Yes."

"And he has driven you off from that place and told you not to slide there?"

"Yes."

"You knew that the policeman did not want you to slide down there?"

"He told me so."

The object of these questions was to show that the city tried to prevent boys from coasting on Jason Street hill, and that the boys knew this.

John's mother was questioned about her son's injuries and how long it had taken him to recover. At the end of Mrs. Frazier's testimony John's lawyer said, "Plaintiff rests." In other words, he had completed the presentation of John's case.

The judge then said that court would adjourn. Since the trial had begun on Friday, there would be a two-day interval before it would be resumed on Monday. The judge instructed the jurymen that over the weekend they were not to discuss the case with anyone.

On Monday morning, soon after court opened, the two lawyers went up to the judge's desk and engaged in a whispered conversation. When the brief conference was over, the judge said that the jurymen were to leave the courtroom.

A jury is supposed to base its verdict on the facts stated by witnesses. When there are legal arguments by the two lawyers, the judge may send the

jury away so that they will not be prejudiced by
what the lawyers or the judge say.

After the jury left the courtroom, the defendant's
lawyer asked the judge to dismiss the case, saying
that Reinman's negligence had not been proved.
He also stated that the accident was the direct result of John's violation of the law against coasting
on Jason Street. The lawyer said that John's
coasting in a forbidden area made the boy partly
to blame for the accident. If he was, then under
the law he could not collect damages.

After a plaintiff and his witnesses testify, the
judge may dismiss the case—that is, decide in the
defendant's favor—if the judge does not believe the
plaintiff has "made a case." Such a decision may
be given before the defendant presents any of his
evidence.

In *Frazier v. Reinman* the judge said he wanted
to hear what the defendant and his witnesses had
to say. He would then decide whether to dismiss
the case or to continue the trial and ask the jury
to give its verdict.

The judge directed that the jury be brought

back to the courtroom. As soon as the jury returned, the defendant's lawyer called a city official as his first witness. This man was an expert on Utica's rules and regulations. He stated that Jason Street had never been designated as a coasting area.

This was a most important legal point. Since coasting on Jason Street was unlawful, John had no right to be sledding there.

The next defense witness was a civil engineer. He was asked a number of questions about the steepness of the hill, the distance at which the driver should have been able to see John, and how many feet a car traveling at eighteen miles an hour covers in a second. (The driver had stated that just before the accident his speedometer showed a speed of eighteen miles per hour.) The answer to the last question was, "Twenty-six and four-tenths feet per second." Everything the engineer said indicated that the driver could not have avoided running into John's sled.

The engineer had drawn a map of the hill with all the important features shown in different colors. The road was blue, the sidewalks black, the houses yellow. The map was handed to the jury so that they could follow the engineer's statements.

The map was used later when the defendant was giving his account of the accident. He was asked to mark on the map the position of his car when he first saw John's sled. What had he done then?

"I applied my brakes and stopped within a car length. I might have pushed the boy a foot, no more than a foot, when I hit him."

The defendant was questioned longer than any of the other witnesses. But finally his lawyer, John's lawyer, and the judge had asked all their questions.

Then Reinman's lawyer said, "Defendant rests. I renew my motion for a dismissal on all of the grounds stated at the close of the plaintiff's case. It now appears that there was an absence of negligence on the part of the defendant from the testimony brought out by the plaintiff himself."

Again, the judge refused to dismiss the case and stated that he would leave the decision to the jury.

Then the judge gave his instructions to the jury. First he outlined the facts presented by John and his witnesses and by the defendant and his witnesses. Next he explained the law on which the jury was to base its verdict. The judge instructed the jury that if it found the driver had been careless, it must next consider whether John had also been at fault. Had John carelessly done, or omitted doing, anything which led to the accident? If he had, he was not entitled by law to collect any money, no matter how careless the driver might have been.

The judge then said that a boy naturally does not have as good judgment as an adult. He instructed the jury that, when considering whether John's conduct contributed to the accident, they were to take John's age into account.

Finally the judge said, "Now, gentlemen, take the case. It is an important case to this boy and it is an important case to the defendant. Make up your mind where the preponderance of the evidence is, where the truth is between these parties; and when you have made that up, let your verdict follow accordingly. Do not be influenced by sympathy, prejudice, or anything else in the case. We are all human, and any normal man loves a boy.

But when you come into a court of justice and take your oath to decide issues squarely upon the evidence, you would not be doing right to let your sympathy for a boy or a girl or anybody else in trouble or distress sway your judgment in deciding the issues.

"Let your verdict be such that both sides will say when they leave this courtroom they have had a good, fair, impartial decision at your hands."

A court attendant conducted the twelve jurors to the jury room, locked the door, and stood guard outside. Until jurors agree on a verdict, no one from the outside is permitted to speak to them.

In John's case, as in other civil cases, the plaintiff can win only if he proves his case by a *preponderance of evidence.* This means that he must convince the jury that the evidence he has presented is more believable than the evidence given by the defendant.

In a criminal case, the preponderance of evidence is not enough to convict a defendant. A person accused of a crime must be proved guilty *beyond a reasonable doubt.*

Juries base their verdicts on the testimony they have listened to in the courtroom and on the rules of law that the judge instructs them are to be applied.

In some cases a jury may send a message to the judge requesting additional instructions as to the law. Or they may ask that certain parts of the evidence given during the trial be read to them. When a jury cannot agree upon a verdict, it is called a *hung jury*. The members of the hung jury are discharged, and a new jury is called to try the case.

While the jury was considering John's case, the judge went to his *chambers,* as a judge's office is called. When informed that the jury had agreed on a verdict, the judge returned to the courtroom.

"We find a verdict for the plaintiff in the sum of $500," announced the foreman of the jury.

Because John's lawyer had asked for $10,000, the jury's verdict was disappointing to John and his mother. But they were due for an even greater disappointment. Reinman's lawyer filed an appeal for a review of the verdict.

Both the federal court system and the state court

systems include appellate courts. Although a trial court usually has only one judge, appellate courts have a panel of judges. The court to which Reinman's lawyer appealed—the Appellate Division of the state Supreme Court—has five judges.

Courts that review decisions operate very differently from courts that try cases. The job of the appellate judges is to determine whether the trial was fair and whether the verdict was in accordance with the law. They do not call witnesses or hear further evidence. They base their decision on a word-by-word report of the trial prepared by an official stenographer, and on *briefs*—printed or typewritten statements submitted by the lawyers for the plaintiff and the defendant. Often lawyers appear before the court and supplement, by oral arguments, points made in their briefs.

In John's case the judges of the Appellate Division decided that the verdict of the trial court was wrong. They said that John was partly to blame for the accident because he had violated the law forbidding coasting on Jason Street.

But the court battle was not yet over. John's

lawyer asked the highest court of the state to give its opinion. This court, the Court of Appeals, is composed of seven judges. They also said that the trial court's verdict was wrong and that, under the law, John was not entitled to collect any damages.

A lawsuit such as John's is expensive. The lawyers are paid by the plaintiff and the defendant. The government pays the jury, the court attendants, and the judges.

But the money and time spent on John's case were not wasted. Ever since John went to court, the rule established in the case of *Frazier v. Reinman* has been followed by many judges. And it has prevented countless similar lawsuits. When a lawyer knows that there is an established rule which makes it practically impossible to win a favorable verdict, he says to a client, "You can't make a case. Don't go to court."

A Criminal Matter

The detective grew increasingly suspicious as he watched the man dragging a large suitcase down the street. It was almost midnight, and except for the man with the suitcase the street was deserted.

When the man reached the street corner he saw a bench, shoved the suitcase behind it, and sat down. The detective then walked up, identified himself as a police officer, and asked, "Where did

you get the suitcase?"

"What suitcase?" was the reply.

After asking a few other questions the detective decided to arrest the man. At the station house he gave his name as Albert Brown. When the police opened the suitcase they found that it contained stolen articles.

A person who is arrested is not required to give the police any information. If he talks his statements may be used against him. At the police station, Albert Brown kept quiet.

It is illegal for the police to hold a person who has been arrested in the hope that he will confess. The law requires that he be brought before a judge without delay. The judge decides whether the arrested person should be "held to answer" or whether he should be freed.

Often a person who is held to answer is not kept in jail until his trial. The judge fixes the amount of money that will be accepted as bail. After money (or some other guarantee) has been deposited with the court, the accused person is released. If he does not come to court on the date set for his trial, the bail money is forfeited.

The sum fixed as bail depends on the seriousness of the crime. In most states a person accused of murder is not eligible for release on bail.

When Brown was brought before a judge, his lawyer argued that Brown should be freed immediately. He said that the arrest was illegal because the detective did not have a warrant to make it. A *warrant* is an order issued by a court authorizing a police officer to take some particular action.

A warrant is not required if a policeman sees a person committing a crime. Nor does a policeman need a warrant to make an arrest if he knows that a crime has occurred and has reasonable grounds for suspecting that a certain person has taken part in it. In other situations a policeman may not make an arrest unless he has a warrant.

The detective who arrested Albert Brown did not know that a burglary had been committed. Brown's lawyer was therefore arguing that the detective had acted unlawfully and that the stolen articles in the suitcase could not be used to prove Brown's guilt.

A few months before Brown's arrest, the Supreme Court of the United States had ruled that evidence seized unlawfully may not be accepted by a state court.

The case before the Supreme Court concerned a Mrs. Mapp, who lived in Ohio. After her conviction for a criminal offense by an Ohio court, Mrs. Mapp sued the state. She claimed that the police did not have a warrant to take the articles which resulted in her conviction. The seizure of the articles, Mrs. Mapp argued, was a violation of her constitutional rights. The Supreme Court agreed with this argument.

The Constitution provides: "The right of the people to be secure in their persons, houses, papers, and effects against unreasonable searches and seizures, shall not be violated, and no Warrants shall issue, but upon probable cause, supported by Oath or affirmation, and particularly describing the place to be searched, and the person or things to be seized."

This provision is in the part of the Constitution known as the Bill of Rights. It consists of ten amendments all proposed in 1791 during the first session of Congress. These ten amendments list a number of basic rights, including freedom of religion, of speech, and of the press.

Originally the Bill of Rights was binding only on the federal government and its courts. A state court acted in accordance with the constitution and laws of that state.

After the Civil War another amendment, the Fourteenth, was added to the federal Constitution. The first sentence of the amendment extends citizenship to Negroes. The second sentence says that no state "shall deprive any person of life, liberty or property without due process of law." The phrase "without due process of law" has been interpreted by the Supreme Court so as to gradually extend to persons accused of crimes by a state government many of the protections contained in the Bill of Rights.

Albert Brown's lawyer argued that, as a result of the Supreme Court's decision in Mrs. Mapp's case, the articles in the suitcase could not be used as evidence against his client. But the lawyer failed to convince the judge. The case was turned over to the grand jury.

In some states the district attorney—or public prosecutor—is authorized to make an official accusation that a person has committed a serious crime. In most states, a grand jury must make such an accusation. It is called an *indictment* or a *true bill*.

A grand jury functions as a board of inquiry. It is composed of citizens summoned by an order of either a state court or a federal court to inquire into crimes. The word *grand* is used in the sense of large. A grand jury may have as many as 23 members.

A trial jury sits in a courtroom, which is open to the public. The jurors hear the witnesses both for the prosecution and for the defense. A grand jury's session, however, is private. Usually the jurors hear only the witnesses called by the prosecuting attorney. A grand jury may require a suspect to appear before it, but he may refuse to testify. Under the Bill of Rights no one may be compelled to testify against himself in a criminal proceeding. In some cases a grand jury may compel such a wit-

ness to testify. But an unwilling witness must be guaranteed that he will not be prosecuted for any illegal acts that he discloses to the grand jury.

The grand-jury system was developed hundreds of years ago in England as a protection against unjust accusations and imprisonments. Earlier, a king could order the imprisonment or execution of anyone he wanted to get rid of. It was a big step forward when a jury of citizens was authorized to consider the evidence against an accused person, and to determine whether he should be tried or released.

In Albert Brown's case, the grand jury issued an indictment on the facts submitted by the prosecutor. The indictment charged Brown with burglary, grand larceny, and criminally buying, receiving, and withholding stolen property.

Next Albert Brown was brought into court for *arraignment*. This is the time when the formal accusation or indictment is read to the accused person. The judge then asks him whether he pleads guilty or not guilty.

Brown pleaded not guilty.

Arraignments may be postponed if an accused person comes into court and says that he cannot afford a lawyer. Various systems are used for providing lawyers to represent persons unable to pay for legal service. Some states have officials called *public defenders* who provide legal assistance. In other states a lawyer is assigned by the court. There are also private associations which give legal aid.

Brown had called his own lawyer soon after he was arrested. After Brown was indicted, the lawyer applied to a judge for a *writ of habeas corpus*. This is an order directing that a person be brought into court. The judge then decides whether the person has been denied his liberty without due process of law.

When the court refused to grant a writ of habeas corpus, Brown's lawyer went to court again. He asked another judge, as he had asked the first judge, to order that the articles in the suitcase could not be used to prove that Brown was guilty. The lawyer also asked that the accusation against Brown be dismissed.

This time the lawyer was successful. The judge

agreed that Brown's arrest was illegal because it had been made without a warrant. Therefore the contents of the suitcase could not be used to prove that Brown had taken part in a crime. Without this evidence there was no way to prove that Brown was guilty. The judge dismissed the accusation against Brown and released him.

The judge gave the following reasons for his decision:

"A search prosecuted in violation of the Constitution is not made lawful by what it brings to light.

"That a guilty defendant may escape the hand of the law is unfortunate, but this court may not subvert the Constitution of the United States to achieve what may seem to be, in an individual case, a desired result.

"Ours is not a police state. We are a government of laws and not of men."

This judge and Brown's lawyer were both carrying out their legal duties. No matter what his personal opinion may be, a lawyer's duty is to use all fair legal means to protect his client's rights. And a judge must carry out the law.

The basic principle of American criminal law is that a person is presumed to be innocent until proved guilty *beyond a reasonable doubt.* In some countries, a person accused of a crime must prove his innocence. Under the American system, however, the prosecutor must prove the guilt of the suspect.

We take it for granted that a person accused of a crime is entitled to a fair trial. But few people probably realize the extent to which the rights of an accused person are protected. If the verdict in the trial court is guilty, the convicted person may appeal to a higher court. If a convicted criminal claims that he was denied rights guaranteed by the Constitution of the United States, he may be able to carry his appeal all the way up to the United States Supreme Court.

If a court finds a suspect not guilty, but new evidence against him is discovered later, he cannot again be put on trial. The Bill of Rights provides that a person may not be tried a second time for an offense of which he has once been cleared.

When a jury's verdict is "not guilty," it is final.

But a verdict of guilty can be set aside by the judge if he believes that it is contrary to law. In some states a judge who refuses to accept a jury's verdict must order a new trial. In other states, and in the federal courts, a judge has authority to *acquit* the defendant—declare him not guilty.

The prosecutor's job is to present the facts. Although he may state them dramatically, he must be careful not to say anything that may prejudice the jurors. If he makes prejudiced remarks, the defendant can claim that he was not given a fair trial and ask that the decision be set aside.

As an example, two men convicted of robbery claimed that the prosecutor's conduct had made their trial unfair. The appellate court agreed. Even though the judges thought that there was proof of the men's guilt, they ordered that the men be given another trial.

A person accused of a serious crime has a legal right to a trial by jury. But in many states an accused person has the privilege of choosing whether to have a jury pass upon the facts or to be tried by a judge.

Just as in a civil case, a criminal trial begins with a statement of the case against the defendant. The prosecutor (whose role is that of the People's attorney or government attorney) submits his evidence and puts his witnesses on the stand. Sometimes one or more of these witnesses may be accused of the same crime. They testify against a co-defendant because they have had a fight with him, or because they think that by giving "state's evidence" they themselves will be treated more leniently, or for other reasons.

The attorney for the defendant may decide not to put any witnesses on the stand. The defendant himself need not testify. The law provides that he may remain silent. And the prosecutor may not make any remarks suggesting that the defendant's silence is an indication of his guilt.

In some states, jurors not only decide whether the accused person is guilty or not guilty, but also fix the punishment. Or jurors may be authorized to make recommendations. In a murder case the jury's verdict may include a recommendation of life imprisonment rather than the death penalty.

Ordinarily, however, the judge determines the punishment. Laws specify the minimum and maximum punishment that may be given for each crime. It is up to the judge to decide whether the sentence should be the most severe permitted by law, the most lenient, or something between the two extremes.

Frequently judges do not name the penalty immediately after the jury announces its verdict. A considerable period of time may elapse before a judge decides on a sentence that he believes to be just.

Courts That Require "Clean Hands"

Suppose your family owns a house in the country where you spend summer vacations. During the winter the house is rented to a tenant. Surrounding the house are many trees which are worth a good deal of money.

Now suppose that the tenant feels that the trees interfere with the view—and starts to chop them down. There are two things your father can do.

He can wait until all the trees are cut down and then sue the tenant for the damage. This would be an ordinary law suit brought under the rules of the common law.

Or your father can go to court and ask the judge to order the tenant to immediately stop destroying the trees. Since your father's chief aim is to safeguard his trees, he asks the court to issue a stop order. Lawyers call such an order an *injunction*. A person who disobeys an injunction is in contempt of court and may be fined or sentenced to jail or both.

The legal procedure for obtaining an injunction is known as an *action in equity*. Equity is a special branch of the law. It was developed long ago to provide legal remedies that the common-law courts could not provide.

In addition to cases asking for injunctions, many others are classed as actions in equity. To understand the difference between the two branches of law—one known as the common law and the other as equity—it is necessary to know something about the operation of the courts in ancient England.

In olden times English judges were bound by many strict and rigid rules as to what they could and could not do. No matter how just a man's case, he could not get help from the judge unless his case came within one of the rules of the common law.

But the king was not bound by any rules. Because he was king he could do as he thought right. Many Englishmen, particularly noblemen, who had cases which did not fit into the rules of common law went to the king to get justice.

In the beginning the king himself probably made the decisions. However, as time passed, so many people petitioned the king for help that he could not handle all the work. The king therefore asked his chief adviser, the chancellor, to assist him. Since the chancellor was acting for the king, he became known as the keeper of the king's conscience. The chancellor, like the king, had unlimited power to issue any type of order necessary to produce a just result.

For instance, when a man who owned land or a house wanted to borrow money, he put up his property as a guarantee that he would repay the loan. The borrower said, in effect, to the lender, "If I do not repay you on a certain date, you will become the owner of my land." If the borrower could not pay the debt on the day agreed upon, the lender took the property, even though it might be worth many times the amount of the loan. The contract—or the *mortgage,* as we call it today— gave the lender the right to the property.

If a week later the borrower obtained enough money to repay his debt, there was no way by which the ordinary law courts could help him to get back his land. The judges of those courts had to say, "You made a contract. On the due date you could not pay. So, in accordance with the terms of your contract, you lost your land."

But the borrower could go to the king's chancellor, tell him the story, and ask his help. The chancellor could say, "It isn't fair that you should lose your valuable property for a small loan. I will issue an order that when you repay the money, the lender must return your land. If he refuses, I will punish him."

Many of the first petitions to the chancellor posed problems that were entirely new. Each was decided on its own merits. Later, chancellors like other judges were guided by decisions that previously had been made in similar cases.

For hundreds of years there were both chancellor's courts (called courts of equity) and law courts. People went to the law courts with certain problems and to the chancellor's courts with other problems.

This system was brought to the American colonies. Many states continued for a long time to operate separate courts for law cases and for equity cases. But today, in federal courts and in most state courts, the same judges decide both types of cases. The judges may act either as a court of law or as a court of equity according to the type of relief that is requested.

But there is still one very important difference in the handling of equity cases and common-law cases. In equity cases there is no right to a trial by jury. When the king was passing on petitions, he alone decided. And when a judge is asked to apply the rules of equity, the decision is up to him.

A basic rule of equity is that the person asking for justice must himself have done nothing wrong. As lawyers say, the plaintiff must come into court "with clean hands."

A few years ago, one professional football team brought a suit in equity against another professional football team. Team A, the plaintiff, claimed that it had signed a contract with a famous college player before Team B had made a contract with him. Team A asked the court to forbid the player to join Team B.

Team A had signed up the player while he was starring in college football. If it had become known that the player had signed the contract, he could not have continued as an amateur player on his college team. This meant that he could not have taken part in a post-season game scheduled for January 1 in the Sugar Bowl at New Orleans.

Team A and the football player therefore agreed that the contract would be kept secret until after the Sugar Bowl game. The contract was not to be sent to the Football Commissioner for approval

until after January 1.

After the deal was made, the player returned to college and began to worry about what he had done. He decided to cancel the contract and notified the manager of Team A of his decision. However, Team A sent the contract to the Football Commissioner for approval. The player was not informed of this action.

Later Team B offered the player a contract, which he signed after the Sugar Bowl game.

These facts were given to the judge when Team A asked that its contract be enforced. The judge who presided at the trial refused to do so.

Team A then instructed its lawyers to ask a higher court to review the case. But again Team A lost its case. The panel of three judges in the United States Court of Appeals said: "We share the trial court's disgust at the sordid picture too often presented in this kind of litigation." Then the judges stated that a court of equity "must decline to lend its aid to either party to a transaction that in its inception offends concepts of decency and honest dealing, such as the case before us."

The judges were applying the rule of equity that the plaintiff must come into court with clean hands.

People sometimes do things which are perfectly legal but which may lead to cheating later on. Such possibly dangerous acts can be stopped by a court of equity.

For example, an association of rare-stamp dealers applied to a court of equity for an order forbidding a company to put a mark on postage stamps to make them look imperfect. Collectors pay high prices for stamps which have been accidentally marred while being printed by the government. The stamps which the company marred were being offered at a quite low price.

In offering the stamps for sale, the company described them fully and accurately. It stated that the markings were unofficial. No one could say that the company was breaking any law.

Yet the judge ordered the company to stop selling the unofficially marred stamps. The reason he gave was that people who bought them might resell the stamps without disclosing how they had been made imperfect. The company was committing no fraud, but it was making it easy for others to do so.

Under the rules of equity, a stop order may be issued before a full trial has been held and all the facts have been proved. This is a *temporary injunction*. Later, after a trial, the injunction may be made permanent.

The stamp case illustrates the usefulness of temporary stop orders. If the unofficially marred stamps might result in fraud, the sale of the stamps had to be stopped immediately. It would be of little practical value to forbid the sale of the stamps after a number of them had been purchased by traders.

Honest mistakes are sometimes made when preparing a written contract, with the result that it does not state the agreed terms. In such situations, a court of equity may *reform*—that is, correct—the contract.

And under the rules of equity, a person who wishes to cancel a contract may in some cases be ordered to go through with it. Such situations sometimes arise in sales of real estate. Mr. X agrees to sell his house to Mr. Y and they sign a contract. However, before the date set for the legal transfer of the house, Mr. X changes his mind about selling and sends back Mr. Y's deposit.

If Mr. Y could buy a similar house for the same price as he had agreed to pay Mr. X, he would not have lost any money. Therefore, under the rules of the common law Mr. Y may not bring a suit against Mr. X. Generally the common-law courts award only money damages. But what Mr. Y wants is the house, and he is ready to pay the full price the contract calls for. In order to force Mr. X to live up to his agreement, Mr. Y brings an action in equity. The court may order the unwilling seller to carry out his agreement.

When the United States Constitution was drafted, it provided that federal courts would rule on law and equity. The Supreme Court, the highest court of the nation, is not only a court of law but also a court of equity.

The United States Supreme Court

The white marble United States Supreme Court building is one of the show places of our national capital. Above the main entrance to the Court is the short inscription, "Equal Justice Under Law." These four words sum up America's legal tradition.

The Supreme Court of the United States is the final authority on what is permitted, and what is forbidden, by the United States Constitution and by

other federal laws. When federal laws are involved,
the Supreme Court has the right to review decisions
of all other courts. It also determines whether laws
passed by Congress and other legislative bodies are
constitutional—that is, in agreement with the Constitution of the United States.

In 1796, only six years after the Supreme Court
was organized, it asserted its authority to determine
the legality of a law enacted by Congress. The law
provided for a tax on carriages. The question was
whether the Constitution gave the federal government the right to impose such a tax. The Supreme
Court said that it did.

At the time few people recognized the importance of the decision. A small federal tax on carriages seemed a trifling matter. But with the
carriage-tax decision the Supreme Court established
its power to decide whether a law is permitted or
prohibited by the United States Constitution.

Today we accept the right of the Supreme Court
to say if a law is constitutional or unconstitutional.
And we also accept the fact that the Court may
even determine whether the President of the

United States has exceeded his lawful authority. In 1952, the Secretary of Commerce, acting under an order of President Harry S. Truman, seized steel mills to prevent their shutdown by a workers' strike. When the Supreme Court decided that the presidential order was illegal, the steel mills were immediately returned to their owners.

In this dramatic case, the Supreme Court announced its opinion, and it was promptly obeyed. Ordinarily the Court's rulings are not carried out so directly. Thus, if the Supreme Court reverses a conviction of murder, the defendant is not immediately freed. The case is sent to a lower court, which issues the order for his release.

The rules established by decisions of the Supreme Court are followed by all courts of the nation. When a New York State judge held that Albert Brown's arrest was illegal, he was following a rule made by the Supreme Court.

People sometimes say, "I'll fight this case all the way up to the highest court of the land." Actually, few cases have a chance of reaching the United States Supreme Court. In most situations, review by the Supreme Court is not a matter of right. The Court must be petitioned to pass upon a case.

Of all the applications for review filed with the Court, it accepts only a small number. If the Court did not have the right to choose its cases, it would be so swamped with work that it could not function effectively. As it is, the Supreme Court can concentrate on problems of national importance. Among these were the four cases brought to test the rights of states to maintain separate schools for white and Negro pupils.

In three of the cases, the Supreme Court was asked to review decisions of lower federal courts which had upheld laws of Kansas, South Carolina, and Virginia. These laws either permitted or required segregation in schools. In the fourth case, a Delaware court had ruled that the state law requiring separate schools was illegal. It ordered that Negro children be immediately admitted to schools located near their homes. In that case the appeal to the Supreme Court was made by the State of Delaware. It asked that the order of the Delaware judge be reversed.

Ethel Louise Belton, the first of the children named in the Delaware case, lived within a few blocks of a high school. Under the old system she was obliged to travel nearly an hour to the segregated school to which she was assigned.

The Court devoted days to listening to the facts about the school cases and probing into the situation. The first hearing was held in December 1952. The following December there was a second hearing which continued for several days.

Visitors may attend sessions of the Supreme Court, just as they may those of other courts. However, so many people wanted to attend the hearings of the school cases that there were not enough seats for all. Hundreds of people could not be admitted.

The beginning of a Supreme Court session is dramatically announced by an official Crier who calls: "Oyez, oyez, oyez." This is an old word meaning "Hear ye." The Crier continues: "All persons having business before the Honorable, the Supreme Court of the United States are admonished to draw near and give their attention, for the Court is now sitting. God save the United States

and this Honorable Court." The nine Justices file into the room through an opening in the draperies behind the platform on which they sit.

The center chair belongs to the Chief Justice. The chair at his right is occupied by the senior Associate Justice, and the chair at his left by the Justice with the next longest period of service. The most recently appointed Justice sits at the far left.

The desks of the Marshal and of the Clerk of the Supreme Court are located close to the platform. Boys dressed in blue or grey suits, frequently seen going to and from the Clerk's and Marshal's desks, are pages of the Supreme Court. An appointment as a Supreme Court page is a great honor. In order to be considered for an appointment, a boy must live in Washington, be fourteen years old, and have an A average in school. While employed by the Court, the boys attend the Capitol Page School in the Library of Congress building. Most of the boys continue to work as pages until they finish high school.

A hearing before the Supreme Court of the United States is conducted in much the same way as in other courts that review decisions of lower courts. Before the hearing, the lawyers for both sides submit their printed briefs. When the lawyers speak before the Court, they emphasize the most important points of their case. The Justices frequently interrupt to ask questions.

In the school cases, the basic question was whether the maintenance of separate schools was a violation of the Fourteenth Amendment to the Constitution. Among its provisions, this Amendment states: "No State shall . . . deny to any person within its jurisdiction the equal protection of the laws."

Fifty-eight years earlier, the Supreme Court had held that the Constitution was not violated if "separate but equal" facilities were provided for whites and Negroes. This ruling was given in a case brought by a man named Plessy. While traveling by train through Louisiana, he had been ordered to move from the car in which he was riding into one provided for Negroes. When he refused, he was arrested and found guilty of violating a Louisiana law. Plessy contended that the Constitution prohibited such segregation. In this test case, called *Plessy v. Ferguson,* the Supreme Court said that the Louisiana law was constitutional. The Court stated that there was no legal cause for complaint if separate cars provided for Negroes were equal to those provided for white people.

Like other courts, the United States Supreme Court is guided by its previous decisions. But when old decisions do not fit current conditions, the Court may reverse an earlier ruling.

Absolute secrecy is maintained about decisions until they are announced in Court. To prevent any chance of a news leak, opinions are printed in a private pressroom located in the Supreme Court building. Decisions are announced on Mondays.

In the school cases, newspaper reporters had been expecting the decision for many months. Whichever way the court decided, it would be front-page news. The newsmen had no way of knowing that May 17, 1954, was the Monday when the historic decision was to be announced.

Some of the reporters were in the newsroom on a lower floor of the building when they got word that the decision was about to be given. The reporters raced up the marble stairway and entered the courtroom just as Earl Warren, Chief Justice of the United States, started to deliver the opinion of the Court. It was the unanimous opinion of the nine Justices.

First, Chief Justice Warren discussed the history of the cases. Then he said:

"In approaching this problem, we cannot turn the clock back to 1868 when the [Fourteenth] Amendment was adopted, or even to 1896 when *Plessy v. Ferguson* was written. We must consider public education in the light of its full development and its present place in American life throughout the Nation. Only in this way can it be determined if segregation in public schools deprives these plaintiffs of the equal protection of the laws. . . .

"We come then to the question presented: Does segregation of children in public schools solely on the basis of race, even though the physical facilities and other 'tangible' factors may be equal, deprive the children of the minority group of equal educational opportunities? We believe that it does."

As to public schools, all nine Justices agreed that "the doctrine of 'separate but equal' has no place."

After a decision is announced, printed copies of the opinion are distributed to reporters. In the school cases they wasted no time in relaying the ruling to their papers. And within a few hours the news was radioed to people in many parts of the world by the United States government on its Voice of America program.

The Supreme Court's work on the school case did not end with the opinion. There was still the problem of how to carry out the decision. The Court invited all states with laws requiring or permitting racial segregation in public schools to send lawyers to present their views. Finally, on May 31, 1955, a little more than a year after rendering its decision, the Supreme Court issued an order directing what was to be done.

Chief Justice Warren said that school authorities have the primary responsibility for solving the problems. Then he directed the courts that had originally passed on the cases to hold further hear-

ings to deal with local questions. The lower courts were authorized to rule on proposed plans for carrying out the integration order. No deadline was named. The Chief Justice said that the Supreme Court's decision was to be carried out at the earliest practicable date.

When the school cases were sent back to lower courts, some people wondered why it did not itself complete the legal work. The school cases were handled in the same way as other cases decided by the Supreme Court. The high Court makes a decision or issues an order. Then it sends the case back to a lower court, which is responsible for carrying out the decision or order.

In a few special situations the Supreme Court may hold trials. The Constitution provides, for instance, that the Supreme Court is to decide all disputes between states. Thus in one case Wyoming sued its neighbor, Colorado, in the Supreme Court. Wyoming claimed that Colorado was taking more than its share of water from a river that runs through both states. The Supreme Court decided that Wyoming had a just complaint. It issued a decree restricting the amount of water that Colorado might take.

More than a hundred years ago there was a boundary dispute between the states of Missouri and Iowa. Both called out their troops. But there was no fighting. For in the United States such disputes are decided by the Supreme Court.

Laws Enforced
by Special Agencies

CAB INVESTIGATES AIRLINER CRASH
ISSUES NEW SAFETY REGULATIONS

NLRB ORDERS EMPLOYEES TO VOTE
AGAIN ON JOINING UNION

FCC BANS QUIZ PROGRAMS

Newspaper headlines such as these might puzzle
visitors from another country. Even Americans are

sometimes bewildered by the combination of letters used to identify government agencies. What is CAB or NLRB or FCC?

CAB is the Civil Aviation Board. NLRB is the National Labor Relations Board. And FCC is the Federal Communications Commission.

There are dozens of such boards and commissions, known as *regulatory agencies*. States and cities as well as the federal government have found that the best way to make some laws effective is by the appointment of a special group of men to supervise enforcement. Part of a regulatory agency's job is deciding whether something is, or is not, permitted by the particular law that the agency is entrusted with carrying out. When doing so they act in some respects like courts.

Some agencies have authority over a single industry, others over many.

Thus the Civil Aviation Board regulates commercial airlines. The Federal Aviation Act empowers the five members of the board to develop safety standards, determine whether certain planes are safe or should be grounded, the quantity of fuel that must be carried, and so forth. After holding hearings and deciding how a certain problem can best be solved, the Civil Aviation Board issues a ruling as to what airline companies must do. Such an order, like any law, must be obeyed. An airline that fails to do so may be penalized by the CAB.

The Civil Aviation Board also decides what airlines should fly certain routes. The owners of a certain airline may think that they can make money by flying passengers and freight between New Orleans, Louisiana, and Oshkosh, Wisconsin. But the airline cannot schedule such flights without obtaining permission from the CAB.

The National Labor Relations Board carries out the provisions of the National Labor Relations Act. This law protects employers and employees in many industries against unfair labor practices.

In one case, a union filed a complaint with the NLRB claiming that it had been treated unfairly. According to the complaint, shortly before employees of a large department store were to vote on joining the union, store officials called an assembly of employees and made anti-union speeches.

The union asked that it be given an equal opportunity to address the employees. This request was denied. The employees voted not to join the union.

The union applied to the NLRB for an order requiring another election. After considering the facts given by the department store and the union, the NLRB decided that the election had not been fair. A new election was ordered.

The NLRB may be asked for a ruling either by the managers or by the employees of any organization to which the federal labor law applies. The NLRB may deal with a department store one week and an automobile plant the next.

The Securities and Exchange Commission (SEC) is another federal agency with broad power. The SEC regulates the sale on a national basis of stocks and bonds to the public. If a bakery located in Des Moines, Iowa, wants to sell shares in its business to people living in various sections of the United States, it must proceed in accordance with the SEC's rules. The same is true for other companies, whether they make automobiles or plumbing fixtures.

Although each government agency has its own duties, all operate in much the same way. Take the FCC as an example. Its regulations affect not only communication companies but also everyone who listens to the radio, watches television, or uses the telephone.

When radio broadcasting began, anyone who had transmitting equipment could put a program on the air waves. Two, three, or four broadcasters might transmit on the same channel. The result was that the programs jammed one another. The obvious remedy was to assign separate wave lengths to each broadcaster. At first the U.S. Department of Commerce made the assignments. But it soon became apparent that merely assigning wave lengths did not solve all the problems. Rules and policing were required to keep order on the air.

Congress therefore passed a radio law, to be adminstered by a group of commissioners. Later the law was changed and its scope increased. The Federal Communications Act authorizes the commissioners to regulate all communication systems— radio, television, telegraph, and telephone.

The communications commissioners, like the members of other federal administrative agencies, are appointed by the President with the approval of the Senate. Commissioners of the FCC serve for seven years. In 1962 a commissioner received an annual salary of $22,000. The chairman of the FCC received $27,000. About the same salaries are paid to the men in charge of other federal regulatory agencies.

The Federal Communications Commission is a large organization, with thousands of employees. Its main office is in Washington, D.C.; branch offices are located throughout the country. The FCC's engineering staff is divided into various departments. One monitors the air waves. It determines whether broadcasters are keeping within their assigned channels and are using the proper transmitting power.

A broadcasting company found to be operating improperly may be notified to appear at a hearing conducted in accordance with FCC rules. At a hearing, the broadcasting company's position is something like that of a defendant in court. Hear-

ings are conducted by employees of the Commission called *examiners*. Examiners listen to the facts. Then they send a report and their recommendations to the commissioners, who make the decision.

The Federal Communications Act provides that the commissioners are to issue licenses to broadcasting stations. The law says that when passing on applications, the commissioners are to consider "if public convenience, interest or necessity will be served thereby."

Suppose two companies wish to operate a radio station in the same community. Both submit applications for licenses to the FCC. Because there are only a limited number of broadcasting channels, only one of the two companies can be licensed. Which applicant will serve the public better? The FCC asks the applicants to submit their program plans, data on transmitting equipment, financial reports, and so on. Detailed studies are made before the commissioners decide which of the two applicants will better serve the public interest.

Licenses are issued for a three-year period, after which renewal applications must be filed. At renewal time broadcasters must again prove that they are operating "in the public interest." Unless its license is renewed, a broadcasting company cannot continue in business.

At one time the FCC announced that it would not renew the license of any company broadcasting a type of program which the Commission considered objectionable. Such programs were being featured by all the major networks. Although each of the programs was different, all were based on the same idea. Members of the radio audience were quizzed over the telephone. If they gave the right answers they won valuable prizes—automobiles, free trips abroad, household furnishings. The prizes were supplied by the companies sponsoring the programs.

One of the programs was a musical quiz. First music was played, and then the master of ceremonies made a telephone call to a number chosen at random from the telephone book. The person who answered was asked to name the music which had just been played. Anyone smart enough to know the answer, or lucky enough to guess it, won a prize. He was also eligible to try to answer the jackpot question. Prizes for the jackpot question were worth thousands of dollars.

Another of the quiz programs required the identification of famous characters. The clues were given in a short play. As with the musical quiz the prizes were of great value.

The FCC did not question the honesty of the programs. Its objection was that the programs were lotteries. Lotteries are illegal. A lottery is the distribution of prizes "according to chance and for a consideration." Consideration is a legal term meaning payment of any kind.

The members of the radio audience who took part in the quizzes did not pay a cent to anyone. How then could the programs be lotteries? The reason given by the FCC was that the radio audience paid indirectly by listening to the advertising on the programs. Because no one could tell when the quiz question would be posed, the audience was obliged to listen to all the advertisements.

The Commission said, "When millions of people sit at home waiting for a telephone to ring, that is something of value to stations and the sponsors. That is as much 'consideration' as paying a price in cash for a lottery ticket."

The programs were immensely profitable to the broadcasting companies. At the time the FCC issued its regulation banning the quiz programs, major networks were collecting close to $700,000 a week for putting the programs on the air.

The regulation was announced in the middle of August and was to go into effect on October 1. The networks lost no time in asking a court to decide if the Commission had a legal right to refuse licenses to companies broadcasting the quiz programs.

The broadcasters won their case. The court said that the quiz programs were not lotteries. Since the programs were not prohibited under the lottery law, the FCC could not forbid broadcasters to put them on the air.

The FCC then applied to the United States Supreme Court to review the lower court's decision. The high court also rejected the Commission's argument that the audience was paying for a chance to win a prize by listening to the advertisements on the programs. The Commission had stretched the legal definition of "consideration" too far, the Supreme Court said.

Although it lost the case, the Commission had established an important point. The Supreme Court decision agreed that the FCC has the power to deny a license to any station broadcasting programs that *do* violate a law of the United States.

Military Law

Of all the urgent matters facing the second Continental Congress in the spring of 1775, few were of greater urgency than the adoption of military laws for the American army. Close to 10,000 men were already in the field, and neither civil laws nor civil courts could be appropriately used to handle the disciplinary problems of the armed forces. From ancient times it has been recognized that there must be separate laws for combat forces and for civilians.

George Washington was a member of the committee that drafted the military laws known as the "Articles of War." They were passed by the Continental Congress on June 30, 1775. The American military code was modeled on the one used by the English. And the military courts, like those of the British, were called *courts-martial*.

After the Articles of War had been in effect for a little more than a year, General Washington suggested that they be revised. John Adams and Thomas Jefferson were members of the committee that made the revision. John Marshall, who later became Chief Justice of the United States Supreme Court, was one of the first judges to apply American military law. When he was appointed Deputy Judge Advocate, Marshall was twenty-two years old and a captain in the army at Valley Forge. The assignment was in addition to his battle duties.

The Articles of War gave General Washington, the Commander-in-Chief, power to pardon military offenders or to reduce the sentence imposed by a

court-martial. This power is now exercised by the President of the United States in his capacity as Commander-in-Chief of the Army, Navy, and Air Force. The President also sets the maximum punishments that military courts may impose. The President's "Table of Maximum Punishments" is printed in a manual which contains official directions about conducting courts-martial.

There are three kinds of courts-martial—general, special, and summary.

A *general court-martial* passes on the most serious offenses. Only a general court-martial may impose a death sentence.

A *special court-martial* deals with less serious violations. It may not give a prison sentence of more than six months, or of hard labor for more than three months.

An officer can be tried only by a general or special court-martial. But an enlisted man accused of a minor offense is tried by a *summary court-martial*. The longest prison sentence a summary court-martial may give is one month.

Courts-martial are not permanent organizations.

Unlike civil courts, a court-martial is ordinarily convened each time a case must be tried. The convening officer decides whether the defendant should be tried by a summary, special, or general court-martial. The decision is important because of the limitations fixed on the authority of each class of military court. If a special court-martial is convened and during the trial it is discovered that the offense calls for a heavier punishment than such a court may impose, nothing can be done to correct the mistake. A trial must be completed in the court where it was begun.

In many respects the legal rights of men and women in the armed services are more limited than those of civilians. For instance, under military law there is no trial by jury. And evidence may be seized without a warrant. In one case a soldier was convicted of stealing on the basis of records he kept in his diary. An officer had been instructed to remove the diary from the man's desk and to turn it over to the investigators. It was held that the soldier had no legal right to complain that the diary was used as evidence of his guilt.

But the rule that a suspect is not required to give information that may be used against him is the same for members of the armed services as for civilians. This rule was recently applied after a cadet, enrolled in an officers' training school, was tried by a general court-martial and found guilty of cheating on an examination.

The examination was on map reading, and the same test was used whenever a group of students had completed a certain part of the map course. A sheet containing the answers to the questions had been prepared for marking the papers. The cadet had apparently obtained one of the answer sheets and had memorized it. The sheet contained, in addition to the answers, directions for scoring the examination papers. The cadet memorized not only the answers but also the scoring directions. He wrote them, word for word, on his examination paper. The officer in charge of the examination reported the situation to his superior, who in turn reported to headquarters.

Under military law an investigation is conducted before an official accusation is made. Just as when a civilian is accused of a criminal offense, military law permits a suspect to refuse to give any information that may later be used against him.

The colonel assigned to investigate did not inform the cadet that he need not answer questions. Instead the colonel put the cadet under oath to tell the truth, shouted at him, and made many accusations. Finally the cadet admitted that he had memorized the answers. A stenographic report was made of everything said during the investigation. This report was accepted as evidence when the cadet was tried.

Since the members of a court-martial are not lawyers, they are instructed by a law officer assigned to the court. He outlines the rules of law applying to the situation. During the cadet's trial, the law officer informed the members of the general court-martial that if their verdict was guilty, the law required that the cadet be dismissed from army service. In accordance with this instruction, the cadet was ordered to be dismissed.

In many situations a civilian has a right to appeal a conviction. But asking for a review by a higher court may be an expensive procedure and many people cannot afford to appeal. Under the American court-martial system, every verdict is reviewed.

The decision of a general court-martial is subject to a series of reviews. In accordance with the usual procedure, the verdict against the cadet was referred first to a lawyer on the staff of the officer who had convened the general court-martial.

The staff lawyer must give his chief a written opinion on the trial. The next step in the review procedure is to forward the entire file on the case to a board of review. There are three or more men on such a board. All must be lawyers. A board of review passes on technical legal points. If the cadet had wished he could have requested that a lawyer represent him before the board.

Ordinarily after a case has been passed upon by a board of review the verdict becomes final. But there is still another court that may be asked to give a ruling.

This high court, the Court of Military Appeals, was established in 1951 when Congress enacted the Uniform Code of Military Justice for all branches of the armed services. It has three civilian judges, all of whom are lawyers. Formerly military men were in complete charge of courts-martial. Critics objected that this system did not always assure a fair trial.

The Court of Military Appeals interprets the law and determines if it has been correctly applied by the court-martial. Like the Supreme Court of the United States, the Court of Military Appeals handles a very limited number of cases.

When the high military court agreed to review the decision against the cadet, the judges did not concern themselves with whether or not the man had cheated on the examination. They considered purely legal questions. Should the cadet's confession, made during the investigation, have been accepted as evidence at the court-martial? Had the law officer erred when he told the members of the court-martial that, if their verdict was guilty, the law required that the cadet be dismissed from the service?

All three judges of the Court of Military Appeals agreed that many legal errors had been made in the cadet's trial and they reversed the decision. The most serious error was that the forced confession had been accepted as evidence against the cadet. The court said:

"The right here violated flows through Congressional enactment from the Constitution of the United States. Military due process requires that a court-martial be conducted not in violation of those constitutional safeguards which Congress has seen fit to accord to members of the Armed Forces.

"These safeguards are for the protection of all who are brought within the military disciplinary system, and are not to be disregarded merely in order to inflict punishment on one who is believed to be guilty."

Although the laws of war are enacted by Congress, the Court of Military Appeals has great law-making power. Like civil courts, the military appeals court makes law by its decisions.

The effect of a ruling by the Court of Military Appeals is illustrated by a case in which a sailor had been convicted of being absent without leave. The members of a special court-martial gave the

sailor a heavy sentence. It included a bad-conduct discharge, hard labor for sixty days, and rations consisting of only bread and water for thirty days.

It is a tradition in the United States Navy, and in most others, to discipline sailors by restricting their rations. Our military law provides that "a person attached to or embarked in a vessel" may be given only bread and water "for a period not to exceed three consecutive days."

The convicted sailor was not attached to a ship; he was assigned to a shore base. The sentence of thirty days on bread and water specified that the sailor was to be given full rations at the end of each three-day period. This seemed to the members of the court-martial to be carrying out the law to the letter.

The Court of Military Appeals said that the court-martial's interpretation of the law was wrong. Only a man attached to a ship may be put on a bread-and-water diet. And the punishment is limited to exactly three days and no more. This decision established the rule to be followed by all Navy courts-martial.

Under some circumstances civilians may be tried by military courts. The law provides that "In time of war, all persons serving with or accompanying an armed force in the field" are subject to military discipline. Mechanics at overseas bases, American newspaper correspondents officially accredited to the Army, and civilian seamen serving on ships carrying army cargoes have been tried by military courts.

Civilians living in the United States, who have no connection with the armed forces, may not be brought before a military court. They can be tried only by civil courts in accordance with all the rights guaranteed by the Constitution.

This rule was stated by the Supreme Court of the United States in a famous case that arose during the Civil War. Lambdin P. Milligan was one of a group of prominent men arrested on a charge of obstructing the war effort. Milligan lived in Indiana, which was in Northern territory. The regular courts were open and functioning.

Soon after the outbreak of the Civil War, President Lincoln proclaimed that all persons guilty of any disloyal actions would be subject to martial law and tried in military courts. Milligan was convicted by a military court and sentenced to death by hanging.

Many attempts were made to obtain pardons for Milligan and another man who had been given death sentences. Until June 2, 1865, the very day fixed for Milligan's execution, it appeared that the sentence would be carried out. Milligan had even written a speech to be delivered when the hangman's rope was put around his neck.

The reprieve which saved Milligan from hanging directed that he be imprisoned in the penitentiary for life.

From the time of his arrest, Milligan had maintained that his trial by a military court was unlawful. A few weeks before the reprieve, Milligan's lawyers had petitioned a federal court to order that Milligan be tried by a civil court.

The two judges who received the petition could not agree as to what should be done and they passed the problem on to the Supreme Court of the United States.

The high Court ruled that the military commission was without authority to try Milligan. He and the other men who had been convicted under military law were released from prison. The Supreme Court wrote a long opinion in which it said:

"No graver question was ever considered by this court, nor one which more nearly concerns the rights of the whole people; for it is the birthright of every American citizen when charged with crime to be tried and punished according to law."

Then, in one sentence, the Court summed up the vital role that law plays in our lives. The Court said: "By the protection of the law human rights are secured. Withdraw that protection and they are at the mercy of wicked rulers or the clamor of an excited people."

Some Legal Terms

Acquittal	In a criminal case, a finding that the defendant is not guilty.
Alibi	The bringing into court of a person accused of a crime in order that he may be told what he is accused of. He is then asked whether he pleads guilty or not guilty.
Appeal	Request for review, by a higher court, of a decision made by a lower court.
Appellate court	Higher court which reviews decisions of trial courts.
Arraignment	The bringing into court of a person accused of a crime in order that he may be told what he is accused of. If he pleads guilty, he is sentenced by the judge. If he pleads not guilty, his case is set for trial.
Bail	Money (or a guarantee to pay money) given to a court to obtain the release of a person accused of a crime. If the accused person does not appear for trial, the money is forfeited.

Brief   A written statement prepared by a law-
                            yer stating the facts about a case and the
                            legal reasons why his client should win.
                            In many appellate courts, briefs must be
                            submitted in printed form.

Case law   The law made by courts instead of by legis-
                            latures. Sometimes called COMMON LAW.

Chambers   A judge's private office.

Civil cases   All cases other than criminal cases. A civil
                            case is usually brought by a person who
                            claims that he has been treated improperly
                            or has been denied a right to which he is
                            entitled.

Civil law   Law that protects the private rights of
                            individuals.

Constitutional   Permitted or authorized by the U.S. Con-
                            stitution.

Contempt of court   Any act involving disrespect to the court
                            or failure to obey its rules.

Conviction   In a criminal case, a finding that the
                            defendant is guilty.

Court-martial   A military court.

Crime   Any act considered harmful to the gen-
                            eral public which is forbidden by law

and punishable by a fine, imprisonment, or death.

Criminal cases Cases brought by the government (state or federal) against persons accused of committing crimes.

Cross-examination The questioning of a witness by the lawyer for the opposing side.

Damages The money awarded to a person because of a loss he has suffered through somebody else's fault. For instance, a court may award damages for a personal injury, for destruction of property, or for the breaking of a contract.

Defendant The person against whom a lawsuit is brought. In a criminal case, the defendant is the person accused of a crime.

Dismissal The ending of a lawsuit by a judge because the plaintiff has not proved that his case is legally justified.

District attorney See PROSECUTOR.

Felony A serious crime, such as robbery, kidnaping, or murder.

Grand jury A group of citizens which inquires into crimes and makes indictments. Unlike a trial before an ordinary jury, the hearings of a grand jury are secret.

Indictment	A written accusation prepared by a grand jury, charging that a certain person has committed a crime and describing the crime. Also called a TRUE BILL.
Jury	See GRAND JURY and TRIAL JURY.
Misdemeanor	A crime less serious than a felony.
Opinion	The reasons given by a court for the way it has decided a case.
Petty jury	See TRIAL JURY.
Plaintiff	The person who starts a lawsuit.
Prosecutor	A lawyer employed by the government (state or federal) to act for it in criminal cases. During a trial, he presents the government's side of the case. He may be known as the DISTRICT ATTORNEY, COUNTY ATTORNEY, STATE'S ATTORNEY, or PEOPLE'S ATTORNEY.
Public defenders	Lawyers regularly employed by the government to represent people accused of crimes who do not have their own lawyers.
Search warrant	A court order authorizing the police to make a search in a certain place.
Statute	A law passed by a lawmaking body, such

as the United States Congress or a state legislature.

Subpoena A court order requiring a person to appear in court to give testimony.

Summons A notice that a legal action has been started. In some cases a summons requires that a certain person appear in court on a certain date.

Testimony Information given by a witness, usually in court.

Trial jury A group of citizens which listens to the evidence presented in court and gives its verdict. Also called PETTY JURY.

True bill See INDICTMENT.

Warrant A court order authorizing the police to take a certain action—for instance, to arrest a certain person. See also SEARCH WARRANT.

Witness A person who gives information, usually after taking an oath to tell the truth, as to what he has seen or otherwise observed about a case.

Federal Courts

SUPREME COURT OF THE UNITED STATES

Highest court in the land. May review decisions of U.S. courts of appeals; decisions of U.S. district courts (occasionally); decisions of state supreme courts (when federal questions are involved); or, very rarely, decisions of lower state courts (when appeals cannot be taken to higher state courts).

U.S. COURTS OF APPEALS

Hear appeals from district courts and federal administrative agencies. There are 11 circuits, each with one court of appeals; there are about 77 circuit judges.

First Circuit: Maine, Massachusetts, New Hampshire, Puerto Rico, Rhode Island

Second Circuit: Connecticut, New York, Vermont

Third Circuit: Delaware, New Jersey, Pennsylvania, Virgin Islands

Fourth Circuit: Maryland, North Carolina, South Carolina, Virginia, West Virginia

Fifth Circuit: Alabama, Canal Zone, Florida, Georgia, Louisiana, Mississippi, Texas

Sixth Circuit: Kentucky, Michigan, Ohio, Tennessee

Seventh Circuit: Illinois, Indiana, Wisconsin

Eighth Circuit: Arkansas, Iowa, Minnesota, Missouri, Nebraska, North Dakota, South Dakota

Ninth Circuit: Alaska, Arizona, California, Guam, Hawaii, Idaho, Montana, Nevada, Oregon, Washington

Tenth Circuit: Colorado, Kansas, New Mexico, Oklahoma, Utah, Wyoming

District of Columbia Circuit

U.S. DISTRICT COURTS

Federal trial courts. There are about 90 district courts, from one to four in each state.

SPECIALIZED FEDERAL COURTS

Court of Claims
Tax Court
Customs Court
Court of Customs and Patent Appeals
Court of Military Appeals

State Courts

STATE SUPREME COURT

Called Supreme Court, Supreme Court of Errors, Supreme Judicial Court, Court of Appeals, or Supreme Court of Appeals. The state supreme court hears appeals from state trial courts or intermediate appellate courts. Except for cases involving federal questions, its decisions are always final.

INTERMEDIATE APPELLATE COURT

Only 16 states have intermediate appellate courts. They hear appeals from trial courts.

HIGHEST TRIAL COURT

Called Superior Court, Circuit Court, District Court, Court of Common Pleas, or (in New York) Supreme Court

OTHER TRIAL COURTS

Municipal Court (Corporation Court, City Court)
County Court
Civil Court
Criminal Court
Probate Court (Surrogate Court)
Juvenile Court
Court of Domestic Relations

LOWER COURTS

Justice of the Peace
Magistrate Court
Police Court
Small Claims Court

NOTE: There is much variation in the names and responsibilities of state courts. The more common are listed here.

Index

About the author

Ruth Brindze has served for many years as an assistant to her husband, a practicing attorney, in the preparation of magazine articles and a newspaper column about the law. She is the author of a number of books on boating and the sea, including *All About Undersea Exploration* and *All About Sailing the Seven Seas*. A graduate of the Columbia University School of Journalism, she lives in Mt. Vernon, N. Y.

About the artist

Leonard Slonevsky, a native and resident of New York City, attended Cooper Union. His illustrations have appeared in *The Saturday Evening Post, American Heritage,* and *Time.*

Allabout Books

ANIMALS AND PLANTS

All About Animals and Their Young *by Robert M. McClung*
All About Horses *by Marguerite Henry*
All About Dogs *by Carl Burger*
All About Monkeys *by Robert S. Lemmon*
All About Whales *by Roy Chapman Andrews*
All About Fish *by Carl Burger*
All About Birds *by Robert S. Lemmon*
All About the Insect World *by Ferdinand C. Lane*
All About Moths and Butterflies *by Robert S. Lemmon*
All About Snakes *by Bessie M. Hecht*
All About Dinosaurs *by Roy Chapman Andrews*
All About Strange Beasts of the Past *by Roy Chapman Andrews*
All About Strange Beasts of the Present *by Robert S. Lemmon*
All About the Flowering World *by Ferdinand C. Lane*

EARTH SCIENCE

All About the Planet Earth *by Patricia Lauber*
All About Mountains and Mountaineering *by Anne Terry White*
All About Volcanoes and Earthquakes *by Frederick H. Pough*
All About Rocks and Minerals *by Anne Terry White*
All About the Ice Age *by Patricia Lauber*
All About the Weather *by Ivan Ray Tannehill*
All About Maps and Mapmaking *by Susan Marsh*
All About the Sea *by Ferdinand C. Lane*
All About Sailing the Seven Seas *by Ruth Brindze*
All About Undersea Exploration *by Ruth Brindze*
All About Great Rivers of the World *by Anne Terry White*
All About the Jungle *by Armstrong Sperry*
All About the Desert *by Sam and Beryl Epstein*
All About the Arctic and Antarctic *by Armstrong Sperry*

SPACE SCIENCE

All About Satellites and Space Ships *by David Dietz*
All About Rockets and Space Flight *by Harold L. Goodwin*
All About Aviation *by Robert D. Loomis*
All About the Planets *by Patricia Lauber*
All About the Stars *by Anne Terry White*

PHYSICAL SCIENCE

All About the Atom *by Ira M. Freeman*
All About Electricity *by Ira M. Freeman*
All About Radio and Television *by Jack Gould*
All About Fire *by Raymond Holden*
All About Engines and Power *by Sam and Beryl Epstein*
All About the Wonders of Chemistry *by Ira M. Freeman*
All About Sound and Ultrasonics *by Ira M. Freeman*

BIOLOGY AND PSYCHOLOGY

All About Biology *by Bernard Glemser*
All About Heredity *by Judith Randal*
All About the Human Body *by Bernard Glemser*
All About the Human Mind *by Robert M. Goldenson*

GREAT DISCOVERIES

All About Great Medical Discoveries *by David Dietz*
All About Famous Scientific Expeditions *by Raymond P. Holden*
All About Famous Inventors and Their Inventions *by Fletcher Pratt*

MAN'S PAST

All About Prehistoric Cave Men *by Sam and Beryl Epstein*
All About Archaeology *by Anne Terry White*

THE UNITED STATES

All About Our 50 States *by Margaret Ronan*
All About the U. S. Navy *by Edmund L. Castillo*
All About Courts and the Law *by Ruth Brindze*

MUSIC

All About the Symphony Orchestra *by Dorothy Berliner Commins*